Poems~Poemas

Christina Watkins

Matchstick Literary
1-888-306-8885
orders@matchliterary.com

For David

A David

To Dorene and Bruce
Thank you so much for your
gift of our stay in your
wonderful guest cottage. It
has been so good to be
with you. I hope you enjoy
the poems!

CW

Contents

Indice

photo
Jennifer Watkins

Towards Phoenix

If you go west to Phoenix
you may have to give up green.
So as you go

consider

soft full branches.
Remember berries
bursting in the tasting.

West may yet win you with tumbleweed
sparseness and wind-swept largeness.

You may see sky's starry cover as brown earth's night-
dressed lover. You may learn to love the west.

Hacia phoenix

Si vas al oeste hacia Phoenix
aprenderás tal vez a abandonar lo verde.
Así que mientras te vas,
fíjate en
las ramas suaves.
Acuérdate
de las bayas
deleitándose en tu paladar.

Quién sabe,
el oeste tal vez acabe por atraerte
con sus escasas hojarascas y
su grandeza azotada por el viento.
Tal vez acabes por ver el cielo
sembrado de estrellas
tal como el amante de la tierra morena
llevando sus vestidos nocturnos.

Tal vez aprendas a enamorarte del oeste.

photo
Jennifer Watkins

Wind Whispers

Wind whispers stories of kinship to everything.
Angels descend into ordinary places.
Seagulls and osprey shake their wings and rise.
Pelicans and kestrels drop like shots.
Angels descend into ordinary places.

Egrets and ibis glide forward on stick legs.
Pelicans and kestrels drop like shots.
Comets and other nebulae swirl on unnoticed.

Egrets and ibis glide forward on stick legs.
Seagulls and osprey shake their wings and rise.
Comets and other nebulae swirl on unnoticed.

Wind whispers stories of kinship to everything.

El viento susurra

El viento susurra su comunión con todo el mundo.
Los ángeles descienden a los lugares ordinarios.
Las gaviotas y las águilas sacuden sus alas y ascienden.

Los pelícanos y los halcones se despeñan como balas.
Los ángeles descienden a los lugares ordinarios.
Las garzas y los ibis se deslizan con patas de palo.
Los pelícanos y los halcones caen como balas.

Los cometas y las nebulosas se remolinean inadvertidos.

Las garzas y los ibis se deslizan con patas de palo.
Las gaviotas y las águilas sacuden sus alas y ascienden.
Los cometas y las nebulosas se remolinean inadvertidos.

El viento susurra su comunión con todo el mundo.

photo
David Watkins

The Ancients Say

The ancients say
sky and earth are married.
Breezes and blossoms
volcanoes and tornadoes
are born of their intimacy.
Incessant changing and eternal touching
are part of purpose.
We who touch and part

share a purpose of the heart.

Dicen los antepasados

Dicen los antepasados
que el cielo y la tierra
están casados.
La brisa y las flores,
los tornados y los volcanes
nacen de su intimidad.
El cambio incesante y
la unión eterna

participan en el propósito. Nosotros que nos tocamos y luego
nos separamos compartimos el mismo anhelo del corazón.

Small Brown-Eyed Boy

Small brown-eyed boy
conceived in rapture and delight thrust out of your mother's
womb bathed in water, pain and blood, I dream you.

It is you who trigger the tenderness in your father's smile. It is for you

that your mother softly sings as she prepares supper for you who play
nearby in the dirt sifting your imagination for clues to your promise.
Years later, I read of you in a magazine:
". . . forced into a truck by a group of unidentified
men . . . taken to an empty lot,
tortured, mutilated and murdered."
Was your mother's name Maria?
Was your father's name Jose?

Niño con ojos oscuros

Niño con ojos oscuros
concebido en deleite y éxtasis
sacado fuera del vientre de tu madre
bañado en agua, dolor y sangre,
sueño contigo.
Eres tú quien le provocas
una tierna sonrisa a tu papá.
Es para ti que canta dulcemente tu madre
mientras juegas cerca con la tierra
cerniéndole la imaginación para encontrar
las huellas de tu mañana.
Años después cuando ya eras hombre
leí de ti en una revista . . .
"arrojado en un camión
por hombres sin identidad,
llevado a un desolado lugar
para sufrir tortura, mutilación y acabar asesinado.
¿Se llamaba tu madre María?
¿Tu padre se llamaba José?

photo
David Watkins

Witness

As if I had a gypsy gene
I go walkabout
or on safari.
I'm a backpacker,
even when I'm home
a witness
to where I've been
what I've seen
what I remember
and what is new.

Testiga

Como si sangre gitana tuviera vagabunda
me pierdo en paseos o safaris.

Mochilera soy
aun cuando en casa me quedo,
testiga yo
del mundo recorrido
de todo lo visto
recordado

o es nuevo y desconocido.

This One

This one, this one.
You will care what happens to this one
in ways that will lead you.

This one will be honey in your heart. This one, with the
usual imperfections, will be worth whatever it takes.
For this one you will never count the cost.

This one is in another currency.

Este

Este, éste es a quién cuidarás
y te guiará hacia tu meta.
Este será la miel en tu corazón.
Este con sus imperfecciones habituales
valdrá la pena.
A éste nunca le cobrarás nada

porque no habla el idioma de las monedas.

Far Traveler

For Angelo Stavros Lozano
(born April 13, 2007)

I dream a rider-less white horse in our garden.
He stands knee deep in red and yellow tulips.
His glow is of deepest morning stars.

By his cloak I know he is a far-traveler.

He stands knee deep in red and yellow tulips.
What do those who pass by our garden see?
By his cloak I know he is a far-traveler.

The baby enters the house through our garden door.

What do those who pass by our garden see? The
far-traveler is with us in our sea of stars.
The baby enters the house through our garden door.
I wonder what dreams will light his way?

Un viajero lejano

Para Angelo Stavros Lozano
(nacido el trece de abril de 2007)

Veo en sueños un caballo blanco solo en nuestro jardín.
Parado en medio de los tulipanes rojos y amarillos.
Su luz mana de las estrellas más distantes de la mañana.

Por su manto, yo sé que es un viajero lejano.

El se para en medio de los tulipanes rojos y amarillos.
¿Qué ven los que pasan por nuestro jardín?
Por su manto, yo sé qué es un viajero lejano.

El niño entra a la casa por la puerta de nuestro jardín.
¿Qué ven los que pasan por nuestro jardín?
El viajero nos acompaña en nuestro mar de estrellas.
El niño entra a la casa por la puerta de nuestro jardín.

¿Qué sueños alumbran su camino?

photo of roses
Annabelle Katz

To My Mother

Could we talk about the garden
while we have another day?
Do the roses need more pruning should the chairs be
put away should we speak about next summer though I
know you cannot stay do forget-me-nots need water

should I water every day? I've always meant to ask you what
you wanted me to plant in the corner by the fence where
the sunshine's rather scant. More lovely border flowers

or are the wild ones best? But you really needn't tell me
for I see you need to rest. And you've shown us very well
all that you know best. So rest now Mother rest.

A mi madre

¿Y si habláramos del jardín
mientras vivimos otro día?
¿Las rosas, hay que podarlas de nuevo,
o arreglar las sillas ?
¿Quieres hablar del próximo verano
aunque yo sepa que no puedes quedarte?
¿Las nomeolvides necesitan agua,
debo regarlas cada día ?
Siempre quise preguntarte qué quieres que yo plante
en el rincón de la valla
donde los rayos de sol escasean. ¿Más flores llamativas
en el borde no serían las flores más hermosas?

Pero realmente no necesitas decírmelo, sino que sí necesitas
descansar. Pues nos has demostrado muy bien eres la que
más sabe. Así que, ahora descansa, Madre, descansa.

Necklaces

A woven gold circle hangs on a thin gold wire
around my neck. It was my mother's.
These days I choose to wear this

birth-shaped womb message.

Christmas energy counts
bright and abundant, noisy and messy belonging to
life among living family. My mother knew that.

Most often
I wear a gold cross
shape of what love costs

with a circle at its center.

Los collares

Un círculo tejido de filimentos de oro
cuelga de mi cuello por un alambre delgado.
Era de mi madre.
Estos días elijo llevar este mensaje,
la configuración de la matriz.

La energía de la Navidad vale.
Es luminosa, copiosa, ruidosa—desaseada.
Pertenece a la vida vibrante de la familia.

Mi madre lo supo.

Muy a menudo, llevo un collar con la cruz en oro— la forma
de lo que el amor cuesta— con un círculo al centro.

Did You Know?

Did you know
Mother God is a salsa dancer?
Her spine loves music.

Her hips swing side to side in circles while her gently curved
arms reach high and low wide or tight together, fast or slow.

She keeps time within her sons and daughters in
everyone and everything near and also far as stars.

¿Sabías?

¿Sabías
que La Diosa Madre es bailarina de salsa?
Su espalda ama la música.
Sus caderas balancean lado a lado en círculos
mientras sus brazos dulcemente combaduros alcanzan
alto y bajo, ancho o estrechos, ligero o pausado. Ella manteniendo
el tiempo entre sus hijos y hijas en todos y todo,

cerca y tambíen lejos como las estrellas.

Dancing With Julio

He comes in wearing sunglasses
baseball cap, shorts, T-shirt
sits on the stage
putting on black sneakers
with elevated arches

selects our music.

With his back to us it begins.
We all show up in the mirrors.
Shoulder shrugs
straight up and down.
Shaking shoulders
so our muscles ripple
front and back.
Flexion-extension
plié and reverse-plié
swan dives to our toes.
Hips in four directions
eight counts each side
then undulate circles.
Some wide stepping
arms swinging. Warming up.

We move into
Salsa with shoulders and hips.
Merengue-style walk,
Samba on tippy-toes—fast.

Joy rises, fills us.
We know things
about ourselves and each other, secrets we could not tell
even if we wanted to. We are in phase within and without,
with someone and no-one. We remember harmony.

At the end of the hour Julio leaves the auditorium.
The rest of us drift to the showers and home.

Bailando con Julio

Entra llevando gafas de sol
una gorra, pantalones cortos y camiseta.
Se sienta en la escena
poniéndose zapatos negros
con arcos elevados.
Selecciona nuestra música.

De espaldas a nosotros inicia la clase. Todos nos mostramos
en el espejo: hombros encogidos de arriba hacia abajo.
Hombros agitándose
para que nuestros músculos se ondulen.
Flexión—extensión.
Plié y plié reversé.
Salta el cisne hasta nuestros pies.
Caderas moviéndose en cuatro direcciones,
ocho veces cada lado.
Y luego en ondulaciones circulares.
Pasos extensos.
Brazos meciéndose, calentándonos.

Nos adentramos en el ritmo de la salsa caderas y hombros
perfilados, pasos de merengue, samba de puntillas—ligeros.

Una súbita alegría nos inunda.
Descubrimos cosas,
nuestras propias y de cada uno, secretos
que no podríamos decir aunque lo quisiéramos.
Estamos dentro y fuera del momento,
con alguién o con nadie.

Al final de la hora
Julio abandona la escena.
El resto de nosotros nos dejamos llevar a las duchas

y volvimos a casa.

East Says

East says set the second half of life aside for ecstasy.
What better prospect than to be a dancer?
Some say St. Paul was reading in the roadside shade.

I have begun to feel the urge to drown my books.

What better prospect than to be a dancer?
Wind is handing out invitations at the door.
I have begun to feel the urge to drown my books.

Retreats are being offered in wild-mind.

Wind is handing out invitations at the door.
Some say St. Paul was reading in the roadside shade.
Retreats are being offered in wild-mind

East says set the second half of life aside for ecstasy

El este dice

El este dice reserva mitad de la vida para el éxtasis. ¿Hay mejor porvenir que el de ser bailarín? Algunos dicen que San Pablo leía a la sombra del camino. Sentí la urgencia de ahogar mis libros.

¿Hay mejor porvenir que el de ser bailarín?
El viento reparte invitaciones a la puerta.
Sentí la urgencia de ahogar mis libros.

La mente salvaje ofrece refugios.

El viento reparte invitaciones a la puerta.
Algunos dicen que San Pablo leía a la sombra del camino.
La mente salvaje ofrece refugios.

El este dice reserva mitad de la vida para éxtasis.

Western Dancing

Under Colorado's wide sky
where celebrated priests preside in cowboy boots
and women wear diamond necklaces with their
jeans we see a sign for Western Dancing.

It's just the foxtrot in boots on a dance floor shaped
like a hockey rink. Men move always forward

while women step backwards except for the occasional twirl
when a glimpse of the other view is possible.

Baile del oeste

Bajo el amplio cielo de Colorado
donde famosos sacerdotes predican en botas de vaquero
y mujeres llevan collares de diamantes con sus jeans
vemos un letrero para el Baile del Oeste.

No es más que el fox-trot en botas
sobre un piso en forma de pista de hockey.
Los hombres se mueven siempre hacia adelante mientras que las
mujeres dan pasos hacia atrás a excepción de un giro ocasional

cuando es possible mirar en sentido contrario.

Spaces

Sometimes when I am dancing
I realize there are spaces beneath my shoes
sometimes pink, sometimes blue sometimes yellow or green
spaces. This happens when I have forgotten there is a floor.

Espacios

A veces cuando bailo
vislumbro espacios debajo de mis zapatos
a veces rosas, a veces azules
a veces amarillos y verdes.
Esto me pasa cuando olvido
que hay un piso.

Wild Mysterious

In the open Arizona desert 'La Casa de Paz y Bien' a monk in his rough—spun brown robe salsas up the aisle after the service. He is light on his feet and nearly floating in his love for the dance. We sense his wild mysterious partner.

Salvaje misterioso

En la soledad del desierto
'La Casa de Paz y Bien'
un monje en su burdo hábito marrón
sale bailando por el pasillo después del oficio de la misa

sus pies ligeros casi flotando movidos por su amor al baile
y por la misteriosa y salvaje presencia de su pareja.

photo
Dylan Katz

Close Together

Close together
sky and earth.
Strength and weakness
are reversed.
Winter warmth too deep
for talking.
Springtime ice too thin
for walking.
Deathly hunger.
Living bread.

Wisest travelers starlight led.

Estrechamente unidos

Estrechamente unidos
el cielo y la tierra.
La fuerza y la debilidad
se invierten.
El calor del invierno
es demasiado intenso para dejarnos hablar.
El hielo de la primavera
muy delgado para caminar.
Hambre mortal.
Pan vivo.

Sabios viajeros guiados por la luz de las estrellas.

photo
David Watkins

Love-speak

If I speak when I am angry
winter is in my words.
Ice makes what has been green
brittle and grey.
Words stay clear once they are in the air.
Words are too solid.
So I will keep a working silence
until I can speak with love.

Amor—hablando

Si hablo cuando estoy enojada el invierno está en mis palabras.
El hielo convierte todo lo verde en frágil y gris materia.

Las palabras permanecen claras una vez en el aire.
Las palabras son demasiado sólidas. Me mantendré
en silencio hasta que sepa hablar con amor.

photo
David Watkins

Calling

I hear
birds on branches
calling softly to me,
"Come closer, come over, come in."

I'm here.

Llamando

Oigo
llamándome
los pájaros en las ramas
"Acércate a nosotros, ven, entra."

Aquí estoy.

photo
David Watkins

Peace

It comes now in the wind – fresh, moving the grasses
spreading seeds and unsettling earth to give them cover.

Its fragrance changes as it takes root takes space
and pushes its way up and into the field.

Nothing stops it.

We are the witnesses
and the wind
the wide sky, the sunshine
the moist places
the bright wild green array.

Paz

Llega abrazada al viento
fresco aliento
por los pastos ondulando
y a la tierra revuelta
semillas ofreciendo esparcidas.

Cambia su aroma desde las raices
hasta el espacio arriba lista
y el campo luego germinado.

Nada la detiene.

Testigos somos
y el viento
el cielo abierto, el sol radiante
la húmeda pradaría
y el resplandor del paisaje.

Christina Watkins lives with her husband, David,
in Victoria, British Columbia, Canada.

Christina Watkins vive con suesposo, David, en
Victoria, Columbia Británica, Canada.

In praise for the poems in this collection:

"The two languages stand shoulder to shoulder on adjacent pages, and it is intriguing to observe how, while each presents its subject in a slightly different light, with a different texture and flavor, they touch the heart equally. The poems form a journey in which "wisest travelers" are "starlight led.""

"In this small collection of short, lyrical poems in free verse, written in both English and Spanish, Christina Watkins gently opens readers' eyes to a world that glimmers with radiance of spirit. Without ever using the words "spiritual" or "religious," she lifts the veil of reality just enough to allow the otherworldly concepts to slip in unannounced."

- Kristine Morris, Foreword Reviews

"Christina Watkins' book of short metaphysical poems might remind readers of nimble, compressed forms such as haiku. True to its title, it takes readers on a journey that is grounded in the earthly but offers flashes of the sublime and the transcendent."

"This is a graceful collection that may appeal to readers with an appreciation for the rugged openness of the American West, the Spanish language and the sacred feminine."

- Blueink Review

"It's a book of poetry about the balance of natural forces and the relationships of people living in the space between. There is a balance between the two poems facing each other. She marries the right words in both languages. The poet's natural sense of rhythm, perhaps explaining her aptitude for dance, shines through in her writing as lyrical poetry. The poems have a compelling beat and expressive melody."

- Alison Walker, Pacific Book Review

"The poems are written in free verse with excellent rhythm and compelling structure, whether you enjoy them in English, Spanish, or both. Each poem connects the reader with nature and, often lightly, with a sense of something bigger through dance, motherhood, and a subtle Religious tone. Readers who enjoy nature, dancing, and graceful prose will revel in the journey. This collection has broad appeal and a beautiful rhythm that makes each poem even more compelling when read in sequence. Watkins has composed poems that softly demand notice and deliver a lovely journey for those who read them."

- Olivia Farr, The US Review of Books

CPSIA information can be obtained
at www.ICGtesting.com
Printed in the USA
BVHW021945270322
632318BV00004B/1